Home Country

Home Country

by Cheryl Savageau

Alice James Books
Cambridge, Massachusetts

Some of these poems have appeared or will appear in the
following periodicals and anthologies:

Agni , An Ear To The Ground (University of Georgia Press, 1989),
*The Eagle, The Indiana Review, The Little Apple, The Lobe,
Reinventing The Enemy's Language* (University of Arizona Press),
River Styx, SAIL, Sojourner, and The Worcester Review.

Library of Congress Cataloging-in-Publication Data
Savageau, Cheryl, 1950-
Home Country I. Title
PS3569.A836H6 1992
811'.54--dc20   91-46573
ISBN 0-914086-94-4

Book Design by Laurie Simko
Cover Art by Carlyn Marcus Ekstrom
Back Cover photo by Bill Siegel

*Alice James Books gratefully acknowledges support from the National
Endowment for the Arts and from the Massachusetts Cultural Council,
a state agency whose funds are recommended by the Governor and
appropriated by the State Legislature.*

Alice James Books are published by the Alice James Poetry
Cooperative, Inc. Alice James Books, 33 Richdale Avenue,
Cambridge, Massachusetts 02140.

CONTENTS

Special thanks to the many people who have supported me during the writing of these poems: to Kathleen Aguero, Joseph Bruchac, and Martín Espada for their generous encouragement; to Adelle Leiblein, Anna Maria Paul, Bill Siegel, and David Williams for help with the manuscript; to Sam Cornish for encouragement at a time when I needed it; to Kathy Hermann for production assistance; to Laurie Simko for book and cover design; to Mary Allard for her patience and enthusiasm; to Carlyn Ekstrom for cover art, hospitality and pep talks; to the judges of the 1990 Massachusetts Artists Foundation Fellowship in poetry, who gave me a free year to finish this book; to the Cummington Community for the Arts; to everyone at Alice James Books; to all my friends and family for their continual support and their belief in the importance of stories; and especially to Bill Siegel, partner and companion, who never doubted I could do it.

Foreword

Returning To The Land:
The Poems of Cheryl Savageau

Coming home, in this land we now call America, is one of the hardest things any contemporary poet can do. Perhaps that is why so many contemporary books of poetry concentrate on charting -- with infinite detail and craft -- interior labyrinthine landscapes which bear little relation to external reality. Coming home is not easy. It is even harder when that homeland is no longer on any maps but kept in the memory of yourself and those few others who see beyond the roadsigns and beneath the concrete. Here, where there is now something called New England, not so long ago there was only Ndakinna, "Our Land."

Home Country, Cheryl Savageau's first book, is a chronicle of returning, returning to a land which never abandoned her, even though as is the case with most "Americans" of mixed ancestry, her Native vision of that land has been called into question throughout her life, diminished, and distorted by virtually every institution -- political, religious, social or medical -- meant to maintain her and to shape her into a "healthy and educated citizen." Yet somehow her family and the earth have helped her see in another way.

In a very real sense, "seeing," the physical act of vision which becomes a spiritual experience, is at the center of her poems, as in the poem for her father, "Trees," which contains these sight-shaping lines:

> You taught me the land so well
> that all through my childhood

I never saw the highway,
the truckstops, lumberyards,
the asphalt works,
but instead saw the hills,
the trees, the ponds on the south end
of Quinsigamond...

Instead of focussing on those highly visible elements of western civilization, the roads which cut the heart of the land, the garish signs of roadside commerce, the industries which have as the central purpose the destruction of forests and the covering of the earth with a lifeless crust, her father taught her to see something older and infinitely more alive: "all New England a forest."

But Savageau does not view reality with either blind or selective eyes. In "Like The Trails of Ndakinna," a simple quote from her father gives us a glimpse of a complexity of experience which has to be recognized as one of the hidden mixed-blood truths of America:

We're French and Indian like the war
my father said
they fought together
against the English
and though that's true enough
it's still a lie
French and Indian
still fighting in my blood

That sort of vision is often painful, but it is needed now more than ever. Celebrations of the earth, not through the medium of a reborn "noble savage," but in the voice of a woman of this century who realizes that being part of this world, being heir to more than one blood, neither disenfranchises you from speaking for the land nor means that you must spend a lifetime mourning what you and the world might have been without Europeans, are vitally needed today.

Savageau's poems do display care and craft -- she is a poet who obviously knows the virtue of hard-won clarity -- and her subject matter is not limited to explorations of her Abenaki ancestry. Her voice, though, is that of a storyteller and one can only tell stories well when one has listened to stories for a long time. Then those stories shape every word you speak. I know that it is no accident that the last poem in this abundant first collection gives us the image of a woman who is both Savageau herself and all women who are close to a Native understanding of their real and mythical place on this earth. (By "Native," in this case, I mean one who knows the nature of the land which gave her birth, one who acknowledges the blood which makes her human -- be it African blood or Asian, European, or American Indian.) In "All Night She Dreams," the narrator sees the powerful animals of the three directions in old stories -- the panther west wind, the north wind bear, the moose which is the wind of the east. She feels herself on the back of the great turtle which holds the earth and then, like the first woman to be born and die on earth, she dreams herself returning to the land. From her grave will sprout the squash and beans and corn. But until then, her breath -- and the poems which ride on that breath, a breath which joins with the winds of Ndakinna -- will rise:

> like smoke, like mist
> like welcome clouds
> like some green and beautiful plant.

> - Joseph Bruchac

The Dirt Road Home

Henri Toussaints

When Henri Toussaints
came down from Quebec
his hands already knew
the fine shape of the world
the hungry feel of earth
eager to be sown
the wet hard flank of a mare
the proper curve of a cradleboard.

His hands had eased the young
from sheep and mares
had freed the bound egg
and women
with no doctor about
with the pains coming close
wanted his hands
to navigate the maze
to bring the child
to first light.

Later the husbands would say
come, Henri, to dinner
eat with us, Henri
and they would sit to table
for the coming of new life
demands great things.

Later, much later,
Rosa had cried out
on the marriage bed
and the blood had come
red and strong and not stopping
as if getting were as hard as birthing.
He had soothed her then as if
she were one of his fine
mares, had crooned

Rosa, ma pauvre, Rosa, ma poule,
til she had quieted
and the bleeding stopped.

She brought him his first son
head so small it barely filled his palm
too small to live, they told him
but in the box behind the stove
next to the steaming kettle
and with Rosa's good milk
the boy had thrived.

Still, when Henri held him
he sang Il p'tit, Rosa, he's small,
and so they called him,
though his name was Armand
and he grew to be a man large
of hand and chest,
still they called him Ipsy
from his father.

And others followed:
Marie, called Tootsie, all small,
Eva, 'tipoule, little chicken,
and Peter who was called Bébé,
though there were more born after him,
eight in all, and Baby Alice,
who was born with red curls
and a hole in her heart.

Cold spring nights
the hole grew grave-size
settled in his own heart
mocked his healer's hands.

4

In the kitchen at night
with the oil lamp burning
he placed the fine gears
into the ancient watch.

The priests are wrong, Rosa,
it is not in the heart
that the soul lives,
but here,
in the hands.

Grandmother

Grandmother, you don't know me
but they say I walk as you did
in touch with the earth.

Grandmother, when you met him
did you unbraid your hair?
Nobody will tell me, Grandmother,
what happened to your hair.

You bore him fine white babies, Grandmother,
their cheekbones high, eyes black,
noses never quite European.

Did you love him, Grandmother,
this white man, this cutter
of trees?

He was a strong man, they say,
walked over half the continent,
lived to be two weeks short of a hundred.
He's legend in these parts.

Grandmother, why
are there no stories
about you?
Grandmother, nobody will tell me
what happened to your hair.

When I was a child, Grandmother,
the earth was my body
and I played in the rain
happy as a frog.
And Grandmother, the hurricane
was my raindance
and the trees
sheltered me

and the sun, the sun
made my body
as red as yours, Grandmother,
as brown as yours.

Grandmother, they knew about you.
And Grandmother, they told me my eyes
are blue.
And Grandmother, they wouldn't tell me
your name.
Grandmother, Grandmother,
I was singing to you,
and they cut off
my hair.

Trees
-for my father, Paul J. Savageau, Sr.

You taught me the land so well
that all through my childhood
I never saw the highway,
the truckstops, lumberyards,
the asphalt works,
but instead saw the hills,
the trees, the ponds on the south end
of Quinsigamond that twined
through the tangled underbrush
where old cars rusted back to earth,
and rubber tires made homes for fish.

Driving down the dirt road home,
it was the trees you saw first,
all New England a forest.
I have seen you get out of a car,
breathe in the sky, the green
of summer maples, listen for the talk
of birds and squirrels, the murmur
of earthworms beneath your feet.
When you looked toward the house,
you had to shift focus,
as if it were something
difficult to see.

Trees filled the yard
until Ma complained,
where is the sun.
Now you are gone,
she is cutting them down
to fill the front with azaleas.

The white birch you loved,
we love. Its daughters
are filling the back.
Your grandchildren play
among them. We have taught them
as you taught us, to leave
the peeling bark, to lean
their cheeks against
the powdery white and hear
the heartbeat of the tree.
Sacred, beautiful, companion.

Looking For Indians

My head filled with tv images
of cowboys, warbonnets and renegades,
I ask my father
what kind of Indian are we, anyway.
I want to hear Cheyenne, Apache, Sioux,
words I know from television
but he says instead
Abenaki. I think he says Abernathy
like the man in the comic strip
and I know that's not Indian.

I follow behind him
in the garden
trying to step in his exact footprints,
stretching my stride to his.
His back is brown in the sun
and sweaty. My skin is brown
too, today, deep in midsummer,
but never as brown as his.

I follow behind him like this
from May to September
dropping seeds in the ground,
watering the tender shoots
tasting the first tomatoes,
plunging my arm, as he does,
deep into the mounded earth
beneath the purple-flowered plants
to feel for potatoes
big enough to eat.

I sit inside the bean teepee
and pick the smallest ones
to munch on. He tests

the corn for ripeness
with a fingernail, its dried silk
the color of my mother's hair.
We watch the winter squash grow hips.

This is what we do together
in summer, besides the fishing
that fills our plates unfailingly
when money is short.

One night
my father brings in a book.
See, he says, Abenaki,
and shows me the map
here and here and here
he says, all this
is Abenaki country.
I remember asking him
what did they do
these grandparents
and my disappointment
when he said no buffalo
roamed the thick new england forest
they hunted deer in winter
sometimes moose, but mostly
they were farmers
and fishermen.

I didn't want to talk about it.
Each night my father
came home from the factory
to plant and gather,
to cast the line out
over the dark evening pond,
with me, walking behind him,
looking for Indians.

Ol' Crazy Baker

We thought it was fun
ridin our bicycles past the cottage
where Ol' Crazy Baker lived.
We peddled downhill
as hard as we could
then coasted by
our hands on our heads yellin
Hey, Mrs. Baker, Mrs. Baker...

She never disappointed us.
Even in winter
she'd be out with a hose
spraying the walk in her
yellow cloth coat
and white rubber boots.
Ol' Baker always wore yellow.
All summer long a yellow
sundress
with her skinny freckled legs
stickin out
and a big yellow sunbonnet.
Ol' Baker was crazy for yellow.
Even her sneakers, yellow.
Crazy Ol' Baker.

Crazy Ol' Baker,
she'd spray anyone with that hose.
I remember even grownups
drivin by in convertibles
the radio up loud
and Ol' Baker'd be out with her hose
and let loose right at them.

I remember my father gettin it
through the open window of the Chevy
once

and all us kids cheerin
that Crazy Ol' Baker lady
and my father cussin
about that crazy ol' bitch
and my mother hushin him
and sayin it wasn't her fault.

That last summer I remember
Ol' Crazy Baker came out
without her sunbonnet
and without her yellow sneakers
and with her sundress over
her head
and we all stood around laughin
at Ol' Crazy Baker's
new stunts
til she began to shout
Come on then and get it, Harry,
you bastard.
and policemen came
and stood around
snickerin
and not lookin
at Ol' Crazy Baker
flappin around loose like that
and her skinny legs all
freckled
and Ol' Baker yellin at them
You're all bastards, Harry, they're all
everyone bastards
and she danced around in her loose
flesh
til I remember my mother came
and said to her
Come into the house now
Lillian

In The Fast Lane

At the pool
all the lanes are full
but one. It is
the fast lane, she knows,
but surely the one swimmer
can stay on his own side
she on the other.
She lowers herself
into the water
and starts to swim
sidestroke, slowly,
letting the water
soothe her, trying
to remember not
to compete with swimmers
on either side, their
strong, steady strokes.

As she swims she becomes
ten years old again
sees her pretty teacher
demonstrating on the dock
pick the apple with your right hand
then bring it down to your left
and put the apple in the bucket.
Now she lays her head down
on the water and stretches,
glad for the long lazy glide
in the sun, the water
alive beneath her with
turtles and fish,
the smells of deep summer.

When the man
swims into her
she gulps water rank with chemicals

smells the chlorine, blinks
at the bright lights and noise.
He is yelling at her,
she is in the wrong lane,
has upset his timing.

She sees him from a distance,
his angry mouth and hard body.
She wants to tell him
his spirit too is hard and bruising,
that no amount of swimming
in this dead water
will cure that, she wants to tell him
about the sun, the turtles
swimming in the depths

but she doesn't tell him.
The man keeps on talking
and for a moment
she sees what he sees: a stupid
woman, middle-aged, overweight,
swimming sidestroke in the fast lane.

Like A Good Joke: Grandma at Ninety
-for my grandmother, Delia Lafford Savageau

I have carried her swollen leg
around with me all day.
For seven and a half weeks
she has hidden this,
walking up and down the corridor
sixteen, seventeen, eighteen times,
no blame wheelchair for her.
She lives alone, the doctors whisper.
Last night the swelling became too great.

I have come prepared to mourn,
but she is laughing.
It's not a clot, she grins.
I've got them stumped.
She is proud of this,
her body's resistance
to their probing.
And don't tell them anything,
she says. They'll cut
my blame leg off.

When a bell rings in the hall
I hear myself asking
what's that for?
Maybe someone died, she says
rolling her eyes. She rocks
back and forth, laughing, watching
my face. Or else it's the ice cream man.

I see her disappearing,
her rocking chair edging
toward a cliff she can't see,
but she stops my look-

Enjoy life, my girl, it's so short.
She shakes her head, then giggles again.
Only not for me, she says,
and smacks the arms of her chair
with glee. She carries her
ninety years like a good joke.

My little doctor, she says,
I asked him, Doctor,
how am I made?
Damn good, he told me, damn good.

Leah

When after days of labor
trying to push the baby out
the doctor told Frank
I can't save them both
how lucky for you
that Frank didn't know
what the priests would've said
and told the doctor simply
save my wife.

I think of you now, Leah,
great-aunt, Grandma's littlest sister,
sitting primly on the high-back chair
in the new dress she'd made for you,
bow in your hair, stockings
pulled up to your knees,
high brown shoes laced tight.

Three times you tried
and each time lost
the baby you'd carried
full term, a doctor's blunder
not once, but two times,
and then the third birth,
a baby so perfect, you said,
so beautiful, he lived ten days
without a rectum.

I know you as the fat aunt
who still cooks cabbage for her Polish husband
dead thirty years, a good cop killed
by punks, you tell me, an honest cop,
as if I doubt you.

In every room television light
rainbows your face
through colored cellophane
you've taped to the screens.
As cancer laces your body tighter
and you grow everyday smaller
your bath is littered with tabloids,
tea-bag fortunes are taped to your doors.
There is nothing too bizarre
to be believed or hoped.

Barbie

i. *The Discovery*

It is true she has
perfect bladder control.
But she suspects something
is missing.
Fingers slide over her crotch
and she begins to feel
a fullness, a budding,
a turning inward.
She dreams of caves,
of thickets and thorns,
dark mouths in the night.
Moths flutter inside her.
She wants to split her skin.
She wants to blossom like a rose.
She wants bees to crawl over her,
probing and sucking in the hot sun.
She wants to be the lush wet
forest floor.
She wants to carry the bowl of the sky.

ii. *She Worries About Her Hips*

Her hips have begun to spread,
there's no denying it.
Now that she's taught her legs to bend,
to open wide in the night,
her buttocks have built a firmer cushion.
Her jeans no longer fit.
Her thighs grow strong.
At the dark of the moon,
they are covered with blood.

iii. *Her Hair*

Short, long. Blond, red,
black, brown. All her life
she's sat with a bubble on her head
in rollers, rags, pins,
with lotions and creams that stung
her scalp, and sprays
that made it hard to breathe.
One day, she shaves it all off.
Lank or bushy, streaked with grey,
what grows back will be hers.

iv. *Her Feet*

Her grandmother warned her about shoes.
How the muscles would change,
the back ache. Now her feet
want to walk on tiptoe forever.
She forces her heels to the floor,
lets them hang over the backs of stairs.
She will learn to walk again,
letting the whole length of her foot
feel the ground. Feel
the heel touch, the toes grasp
the luxurious roll forward.
She will learn to run.

Somewhere Arms and Legs

When Anita's finger
pierced by the needle
of the new treadle machine
bled, then festered,
when the doctors quit trying
and said cut it off
it's all we can do,
the infection spread to the bone,
it was you who said
No (anita's fingers
dancing over the keyboard)
who said *No* (anita playing
i've got you under my skin)
who said *No* (until she
heard you walk in the door
and the song changed to
won't you come home
bill bailey) who said
No (fingers bleeding,
missing, blood on the keyboard).

No, you said to them
and nursed the finger back to health
with long soaking in hot salt water
and quinine, dressings
you changed yourself each day
coming home early from work to do it,
and to brew the teas that would speed healing.

I've heard this story
all my life.

Pepere, you weren't there
when the doctors spread my legs
and put the tiny shield
inside me, when the cramps came

and the bleeding made me
white and weak
it took me ten months
til I said *No*
and they pulled that invader
that angry tooth, from my womb.
Still I bled babies,
three in two years
clots in the toilet
somewhere arms and legs,
a smile, a pair of eyes,
a child.

I dream an old woman
somewhere in a garden
gathering the harvest
of children. She carries them
in her apron, like ears of corn,
and walks down the dusty road
into the gathering dusk.

You weren't there, Pepere
dead before I was born,
you weren't there
to feed me the healing teas,
you weren't there,
only the story to tell me
to say *No*, to say *No*

Pepere
I am learning to say it
with you
I am learning to say it
without you

At Fifteen Louise Kills Chickens
-in memory of Louise Monfredo

When the order comes in
her mother is on her way to a sister's,
and her father is out haying.
Anyway, this is women's work.
You'll have to do it, Louise,
her mother said.
Forty chickens to the hotel before dinnertime.
Forty chickens plucked and dressed.

Louise holds the chicken in her arms
and swings its neck to the ground.
She places her boot firmly on the head
and pulls.

It's the only way, she tells me sixty years later,
to kill a lot of chickens in a hurry.

She tosses each bird
into the pot of boiling water
to loosen its feathers.
There's blood in the dust,
on her hands, her clothes,
red as her own blood that lately
she has welcomed as her body's secret promise.
But she is not thinking of that now.
She has to work quickly.
The sun is hot, and after the killing
there's more work to be done.

Plucking forty chickens takes time.
She works in a haze of feathers and blood
cleaning the insides, dropping
hearts, liver, and gizzard into one pile,
the waste into a waiting can.

Could you do it by twisting their necks? I ask her.
Oh, sure, if you're strong enough, she says.

As she works, time slips away.
It is just the crunch of the chickens' heads
under her boot, the slippery wet feathers,
the endless sorting and cleaning,
and the smell of blood and fowl.
She is making meat.

My grandmother told me she sang to them first, I say.
Is that possible? Louise laughs. Bet she
calmed them right down, she says.

When she looks up from the last of the birds
she wipes a hand across her forehead,
and squints at the horizon's thin line of grey.
She loads the wagon by herself, hitches the horses,
and goes inside to wash.

Louise delivers the chickens on time,
and remembers to collect what she is owed.
Forty chickens before dinnertime,
forty chickens plucked and dressed.
Her mother won't be disappointed.

And what came after that?
Did she make dinner for her mother's return?
Feed her father and brothers?
Did the sister die or live to bear more children?
Louise didn't say, but I do know this -
Afternoons, when the sky darkened
and blossomed grey
she slipped the saddle off her mare
and rode bareback
to meet the storm.

Hanging Clothes In The Sun

His youngest daughter helps him
wring the clothes
while his wife answers phones
for doctors. The washing machine
is broken again.

In the factory
where he etches pathways
onto silicon chips
he wears a white coat and pants,
special shoes
to protect the chips from dust.

This is the best job he's had.
Better than last year
when he sprayed lawns with poisons,
then set up little signs
warning others not to walk there,
his clothes saturated,
his asthmatic lungs
choking on the clouds
marked hazardous to pets and humans.

All summer, he'd had to refuse
his daughters' hugs until
he removed his poisonous clothes
on the back stoop. Tee shirt,
jeans, baseball cap,
he put them in a plastic bag,
and showered while his skin burned.

Before that it was asbestos.
Wrapped in plastic,
he'd removed the sagging ceilings,
the flaking insulation on basement pipes,
vacuuming to remove the tiny particles

that would lodge in the lungs.
They floated in dreams, followed him
like a swarm of invisible bees.

This job was better than that,
in spite of the tanks of solvents
leaking noxious fumes,
the paychecks that didn't stretch.
Better than working at the defense plant
across the lake, where Air Force personnel
checked his I.D. badge each morning,
where everything and nothing was secret.

He squeezes water
out of shirts and towels.
He knows he drinks too much.
He dreams of moving to New Hampshire,
where his people walked
for 10,000 years,
and where, he believes,
the water is still clean,
but up north, the Lancaster paper mill
spills dioxin into the Connecticut River,
and downstream, five young girls have surgery
to remove cancerous wombs.
Anyway, there's no money.

Now the washing machine
is spewing soapy water
onto the basement floor.
His daughter frowns determinedly
at the towel in her hands.
At five years old, she knows how to help,
squeezing out the dirty water,
hanging clothes in the sun.

Logic Problem

the lesbians are on the third floor
the zippers for men's jeans are mainly on floor two
the directions for filing A.B. Dick are on floor one
the women who are easy lays are on floor two
the men are generally on floor one
the women who secretly agree they have no brains
are on the first floor
the women who are the hope of the world use colorful
language on the second floor
the woman reading Proust in the bathroom is on floor one
the woman who thinks she is a poet is on floor three
the woman who sings while she works is on the second floor
new leather bags are carried casually on floor three
the woman who has had three abortions is on floor three
the woman who had one abortion is no longer on floor two
the pictures of the Blessed Virgin are in lockers
on the second floor
the pictures of naked women are in a locked desk
on the first floor
Mother Jones is on the third floor
but she'd be more comfortable on the second

the woman who is unbuilding her life waits for directions
by the third floor phone
the man who calls in the night for his dead mother rings
for another cup of coffee on floor one
the woman with bruises blooming like roses on her breasts
waters the boss's plants on the ground floor
the man who secretly loves silk longs to visit
the third floor
on the second floor the woman who has had four miscarriages
is taking codeine for menstrual distress
the woman whose son is learning to live without ecstasy
wears only natural fibers on the third floor

the woman on the first floor who is three months' pregnant
visits the bathroom to vomit her boss's smoke one more time
the woman whose husband did not come home last night
sneaks a cigarette in a second floor stairwell
on the ground floor, the woman whose mother is dying
enters the number '3' into the computer 400 separate times
the man whose wife is recovering from a mastectomy
is hunting for breast on floor two
the woman who dreams nightly of vaginal flowers
is not on the third floor

in the harbor waters, luminous fish
are circling
what are their colors?

when birds walk the parking lot
in the grey off-shift hours,
what is the quality of light?

and the singing of stone
that rings through the city -
which of the women hears it?

Department of Labor Haiku

In the winter snow
the kitchens fill up with steam
and men out of work

Why They Do It

Uncle Jack drinks because he's Indian.
Aunt Rita drinks
because she married a German.
Uncle Raymond drinks
because spats have gone out of style.
Uncle Bébé drinks
because Jeannie encourages him.
Aunt Jeannie drinks because Bébé does.
Russell drinks because he's in college.
Uncle Jack drinks
because he's a perfectionist.
Dave drinks because he's out of work.
Aunt Rita drinks
because she's a musician.
Bert drinks because he's married to Rita.
Renny drinks
because he likes a good time.
Gil drinks because he always has.
Raymond drinks
because Marie's too smart.
Jack drinks because Florence won't.
Lucille and Bob don't drink
because everyone else does.
Raymond drinks because of all the women
he'll never have.
Dick just drinks to empty the keg.

Infant of Prague

My mother sews new clothes
for the Infant
who stands on the kitchen table
in his painted plaster robes.
These cold clothes are not enough.
His new robe will be red,
satin, lined with white,
and trimmed with metallic gold
rick-rack. Underneath,
he'll wear a long white dress,
embroidered with red and gold
crosses. More beautiful
than my brother's christening dress,
and shinier. She tries it on him,
warns me away,
this is not a doll, no toy
for me to dress and undress.
The infant stands
patiently
as she tries on the robe
and sews the scratchy lace
around his neck and wrists.
He doesn't fidget or cry
the way I do
when she fusses with my
hair and clothes. He is
a good child.

He holds a blue ball in his hands.
Ma tells me it is the world
but all I see is the sharp cross
growing out of the top, sure to
poke out an eye, cut
his pretty mouth when he falls.

The Sound of My Mother Singing
-for my mother, Cecile Meunier Savageau

He drops a motor
on the dining room table,
bellows at the big girls.
Rita plays the piano
while Florence cries.
When he waves the butcher knife
in their mother's direction,
Eva pretends to faint
on the theory that no one
will hurt a sick person.

Outside, Bertha sneaks a smoke
under the stairs.
In the basement, Bébé holds
his pet rabbit inside his shirt.
There, he says, don't worry.
Pa won't hurt you.
He pets the silky fur,
feels the comfort of claws
and twitching nose against his chest.
Don't worry, don't worry.

Crouched behind the bedroom door,
Lucille, the youngest one, my mother,
watches through the crack.
Her mother moves silently
around the kitchen.
Her oldest sister, Marie,
puts food in front of her father,
fork, spoon, butterknife.
She pours coffee.
Slouched over his plate,
he has forgotten his rage,
forgotten the butcher knife,
and Marie slips it into a drawer.

Lucille watches him eat,
thick slices of cheese and onions,
a plate of steak and eggs.
Where is the redhead? he says,
looking up from his food.
Come, tête-rouge, he calls,
viens, viens.
He is speaking to her
from under his armpit,
head down, smiling
toward her hiding place.

She hears her mother speaking,
Stop, Henri, you frighten her.
But now he is waggling his fingers,
smiling at her. This
is her Pa's face.

Lucille sits on his lap
as he eats, it will be all right now,
he is smiling, he loves her,
his little tête-rouge,
she can make him smile.

Late in the night
she is awakened by Marie,
who carries her outside in her nightie.
Florence and Eva wait for them
behind the lilacs. Lucille
sees movement behind the shed
and waves to Bébé and Rita.
She likes this nighttime game
of hide and seek.

When Pa comes out of the house,
Lucille is wide awake. She leans forward
to call out to him. Here we are Pa,

she wants to say. She feels
Marie's hand over her mouth and remembers
not to talk.

In her father's hand the blade
reflects the moonlight.
Come out, les enfants, come out, he calls.
His voice is soft, cajoling
in the warm night.
Come out, children, come out, he croons,
so I can kill you.

In the office
Lucille types.
She brings coffee, arranges calendars,
cleans desks. She smiles often.
Her boss calls her Red. She is the favorite.
Soon she is calling banks, investing money
for the company, forgetting it isn't her own.
They tell her how good she is. She sings
she flirts, she keeps them smiling.

Sing for me, tête-rouge,
her father says.
So she sings a song
he taught her
and he sings with her
that's right, that's right
sing some more
and she keeps on singing
while her mother cleans up
and her sisters watch.

One day she is let go. No degree, they tell her.
No one without a degree can do this job.

It is not clear
when the change comes,
when his hands become cruel
on her arms. He is saying over and over
You love your Pa? Hanh? You love your Pa?

She is crying. She has done something wrong.
She is trying but
she can't
sing
anymore.

The Water Flowing Through Me

Beaver Woman

I carry black mud in my mouth
It is the mud of my grandmothers
I carry black mud to the lodge
I do this again and again
I carry black mud of my grandmothers
In my mouth I carry it

Come
swim this water
haul the perfect log home

I carry black mud in my mouth
It is the mud of my grandmothers
I carry black mud to the lodge
I do this again and again
I carry black mud of my grandmothers
In my mouth I carry it

Come
swim through these doorways
strip bark for the tender green inside

I carry black mud in my mouth
It is the mud of my grandmothers
I carry black mud to the lodge
I do this again and again
I carry black mud of my grandmothers
In my mouth I carry it

Come
swim this water
already your back is glistening

What I Save

Like my grandmother now, I save teabags for a second
cup. String, stamps without postmarks, aluminum foil.
Wrapping paper, paper bags, bags of scrap fabric,
blue rubber bands, clothes hangers. I save newspaper
clippings, recipes, bits of yarn, photographs in
shoeboxes, tins of buttons. I save cancelled checks,
instruction manuals, warranties for appliances
long-since thrown away. Feathers, shells, pebbles,
acorns. I save faces, phrases, bits of melody, the
light on the trees from a late autumn day. I save
my grandmother's hair, carefully braided and coiled
in tissue paper. I save the moment my infant son
nuzzled my breast and began to suck. I save my lover's
hands touching me. I save his tongue, his teeth.
I save the strong smell of sex. I save the rhythm.
I save the sound of geese flying overhead, the smooth
young bark against my cheek, the white dust of birch
on my hands.

I save the water flowing through me
that cannot be contained.

Equinox: The Goldfinch

it is as if he had swallowed the sun
which slept the winter inside him
until he forgot what it was like
to live in warmth, and golden.
but his body has the knack of timing.
for weeks now golden feathers
have appeared among the grey and khaki brown
now his back is mottled with ice floes
drifting in water that is not blue
but shining purest yellow

he rides upon the cusp of winter
and he is full of sun
it is too much for him to bear
his throat swells with it
and he pushes the sun out
into the air where it turns
immediately to song. The notes

fall back to him, and he tries again,
head back, throwing the sun
into the air, and it returns
to him, and yet again,
and again, there is no end
to this light that is filling him,
it is the sun he has become the sun.
his song shimmers with light
and his body blossoms
into yellow

Summer Solstice

For seven days I heard the cat
as she padded full-pawed
up the driveway,
crying steadily as she walked,
as if she were calling kittens
or a mate.

She stopped beneath the Japanese maple,
the place she'd chosen
to drop the tiny mouse
I hadn't seen she was carrying.

The mouse crouched in front of her
stunned or hypnotized,
and the cat looked around,
and began to sing.

Her voice rose and fell
in all the inflections known to cats.
The rolling tones that start deep in the throat
then open into invitation, the inquisitive hum
she'd used when nuzzling kittens, the demanding wail
I'd gotten used to hearing outside the kitchen door.

The mouse,
delicate-boned, velvet-furred,
never moved, never twitched
an ear or hair.

This went on for some time.
It was a very small mouse,
maybe born this spring
before the grasses bloomed.

I don't know how long exactly I watched,
but long enough for me to think

she doesn't really want the mouse,
long enough that in a fit
of human misunderstanding
I thought to save the mouse,
and walking toward them,
spoke the cat's name.

She looked up,
her eyes intent and distant,
then calmly picked up
the waiting mouse
and with one sure bite,
bit off its head and ate
bones and fur and all,
until there was nothing left
but a drop of blood
on her whiskery brow.

For seven days she did this
an hour or two before sunset
and after that first day I watched
from wherever the cry caught me,
surprised each time
by ceremony.

There is a love between hunter and prey
that I am just beginning to understand.

On the threshold of summer,
beneath the red-leafed tree,
she sang the terrible song
that turns the seasons.
And the earth, having its fill of light,
turned again toward darkness.

Bones - A City Poem

forget the great blue heron flying low
    over the marsh, its footprints
    still fresh in the sand

forget the taste of wild mushrooms
    and where to find them

forget lichen-covered pines
    and iceland moss

forget the one-legged duck
    and the eggs of the snapping turtle
    laid in the bank

forget the frog found in the belly of a bass

forget the cove testing its breath
    against the autumn morning

forget the down-filled nest
    and the snake swimming at midday

forget the bullhead lilies
    and the whiskers
    of the pout

forget walking on black ice
    beneath the sky hunter's bow

forget the living waters
    of Quinsigamond

forget how to find the Pole star and why

forget the eyes of the red fox
  the hornets that made their home
  in the skull of a cow

forget waking to hear the call of the loon

forget that raccoons are younger brothers
  to the bear

forget that you are walking
  on the bones of your grandmothers

The Sweet and Vinegary Taste
- for my grandmother, Rose LeBlanc Meunier

Summer overflowed the kitchen
where Memere made pepper relish
and picalilli,
cooked up tons of beans,
and served us cucumbers and tomatoes
three times a day.

Every morning I followed her
down the cellar stairs
and out the back door
a load of laundry in her arms,
a bag of clothespins in mine.

A big girl now,
I grabbed the pole
and lowered the clothesline.
I hung the little things,
socks, underwear,
while Memere hung the sheets.

The line heavy with clothes,
Memere helped me push the pole
until the sheets swung
above my head,
closer to the wind, Memere said,
and safe from dogs.

But laundry was just an excuse.
The garden was what pulled us out,
and after clothes were hung
we walked our usual path
in and out among the beans and squash,
pulling a weed here, flicking a caterpillar
from the tender vines.

We buried fish
to make the plants grow.
We tied tin pie plates to strings
to keep the birds away, and
Memere wasn't bothered if
it didn't work. Birds flew
above and walked through the corn.
When I raised my arms and ran
to chase them Memere's voice would come,
Bury the fish, she said, and let the birds be.

Her knobby hands
working in the dark brown
New England soil
never seemed to doubt
there'd be enough.
This piece of earth
we called garden
was home, she knew,
to many, and not ours alone.

Bury the fish and let the birds be,
she said. There will be enough.

And there was enough.
Enough for everybody,
for birds, and rabbits,
and caterpillars, enough
and more than enough
to overflow the kitchen,
to fill the winter shelves
with the sweet and vinegary taste
of life, the mystery
flowing from the earth
through her hands
to our open mouths.

Charm For A Sister With Child

tonight I sort
the crimson berries
to put into the bread
I bake for you, my sister

thin slices, four-chambered
tart and seeded with
new life, your heart
will know them, sister

the oranges I cut in half
and press for juice in the old way
this juice like sun quickening the bog
this morning gold I add for you

and honey that the tart and sweet
be wedded well, and walnuts whose black dye
made dark my hands and yours
revealing secret names

and eggs I add for binding

when the air is deep in oven smells
the bread rises golden, brown, and crisp
I deliver it from the heat
wrap it carefully in cool linen

these loaves I make
and bring to you, sister
we spread the slices thick
with cream, and eat

your roundness grows in me
and we are heavy with waiting
as we share these loaves, this
life, this child you shine

Comes Down Like Milk

My mother's curls
have come undone.
She washes her mother's legs
and covers them
in clean sheets.
When we lean over
to turn her shrunken body
Memere takes a sharp breath.
My mother and I become still,
our bodies grow bigger
trying to absorb the pain.

We wait for the soft moan.
Instead, Memere grasps
the braid running down my back.

While I adjust the pillow,
my mother gets comb and brush.
Together we take out the pins.
Memere's hair comes down like milk.

For The Woman Who Died In The Deer Park

Today the air presses
as if before a storm.
The air has never failed her in this,
alerting her with fresh winds,
swaddling her with moist breath.
She knows change from the shift of air
on her cheek, knows change
like the passing of a hand.

She expands with each step,
until she feels herself in each tree,
moss growing on her sides,
the taste of lichens in her mouth.
She walks past the children,
not seeing them,
an old woman in white nightdress,
braid hanging to waist,
walking with bare feet.

The bare rock rises from the grass,
like knees and elbows.
She wants to lie on this green blanket
and hear the songs her mother taught her.
She kneels, puts her ear to the ground.
The earth is singing faintly.
She lies on her side,
listening, her face pressed close,
the grass rising around her.

She hears a sound, like
the rush of wind through the woods,
like her own breath. But the breathing
is not hers.
The deer stands above her
like a forest, a dark hill.

The deer. She'd forgotten
the deer.

She puts out her hand.
The song is all around her now.
The deer bends his head
and she rises toward him.
His breath covers her,
warm and sweet.
She breathes him in,
the song rising inside her,
and the earth singing with her,
Coming home, coming home.

Mother Night: Full Moon Past Solstice

Tonight you lie on your side
extending your black body
past all seeing
and the earth, just one
in a litter of planets,
turns toward you,
and you bare your breast
to the winter night.

       Look, my husband says,
       there's a ring around the moon.

But no moon ring
ever filled my eyes like this,
from horizon to horizon,
and I press my face
against the night
and curl my fingers
into clouds
as I breathe in the cold winter sky
and wrap my lips around the moon.
What I taste are sweet
stars that fly spinning
and sparking against my teeth.
Soon entire galaxies
are flying down my throat
until the whole night is whirling
and pulsing inside me and I pull back
satisfied and smile,
thank you, Mother,

       Ice crystals, he explains,
       Yes, I say

and lick the stars from my lips.

Scene from Morrisseau: Woman Suckling Bears

her breasts are brick-red
and point to earth
golden bear-children suckle,
their arms like sickle moons.
one balances her breast on his claws,
the other nips her with sharp teeth,
his dark paw searching her side.

with one golden arm, she reaches down,
caresses the shaggy belly
of the one who reclines.
she draws the standing one closer.
they are joined by spider threads.

she looks away over their heads.
she is weeping.
from her brow, her hair leaps,
a black thunderbolt.
around them,
the world turns white.

Medicine Woman
-for Dovie

medicine woman they call me
as if I should like it
like the kids in school
who called me little white dove
from some stupid song
about one more Indian woman
jumping to her death
how come you have an animal name?
they asked me, how come?
and I went home to ask my father
how come, Dad, how come
I have an animal name?

now white women come into my shop
and ask me to bless their houses
(what's wrong with them, I want to ask)
name their grandchildren
(do I know your daughters?)
blow some smoke around
say some words, do
whatever it is you do
we want someone spiritual-
you're Indian, right?

right. my tongue is held
by their gray hair
they are grandmothers
deserving of respect
and so I speak
as gently as I can
you'd let me, a stranger,
come into your home, I ask
let me touch

your new grandchild
let me name
the baby
anything
that comes into my head?
I am not believing this
but they are smiling
and tell me again
we want someone
spiritual
to do it

I write to my father
how come you never
told me who we are, where
we came from?

Women keep coming into my shop
putting stones in my hands
Can you feel that? they ask
Of course I can feel it
I'm not dead, but that
is not the right answer

My father writes back
the garden is doing good
the corn is up
there's lots of butterflies
all I know is
we come from the stars.

To Human Skin

My father's eyes were blue
like his grandfather's
but if I trace the line
of nose and chin
it is his grandmother's face
I see. Abenaki woman.

His heart was green and growing,
as if he'd lived for centuries,
an old forest tree man
rooted in the rocky soil
now called new england,
as if Gluscabe's arrow
had just pierced the bark
and turned it to human skin.

Ndakinna, I want to tell him now.
Ndakinna. There is a name
for this place you call in English
the home country.

Over the last meal
we'll ever eat together
he tells me, I'm going up north,
up to the old home country,
Abenaki country. He smiles
in anticipation, his feet
already feeling the forest floor,
while my stomach tightens
with the knowledge that he
is going home. I push
the feeling away. But when spirit
talks to spirit, there is no denying.

Through the long days of mourning,
I see my father's spirit
walk into the bright autumn woods.
Red, gold, and evergreen,
they welcome him back,
his relatives, green of heart,
and rooted, like him,
in the soil of this land
called Ndakinna.

At The Pow Wow

my mother, red-haired,
who lived with my father
forty years,
who buried my grandparents,
whose skin was brown, she said,
from age,
watches the feathered dancers
and says, so that's
what real Indians look like.

I wrap the shawl around my shoulders,
and join the circle.

Like the Trails of Ndakinna

We're French and Indian like the war
my father said
they fought together
against the English
and although that's true enough
it's still a lie
French and Indian
still fighting in my blood

The Jesuit who traveled up the St. Lawrence
found the people there uncivilized
they will not beat their children
he wrote in his diary by candlelight
and the men listen too much
to their wives

You who taught me to see no borders
to know the northeast as one land
never heard the word Ndakinna
but translated without knowing it
our country, Abenaki country

Grandmothers and grandfathers
are roaming in my blood
walking the land of my body
like the trails of Ndakinna
from shore to forest

They are walking restlessly
chased by blue eyes and white skin
surviving underground
invisibility their best defense

Grandmothers, grandfathers,
your blood runs thin in me
I catch sight of you
sideways in a mirror
the lines of nose and chin
startle me, then sink
behind the enemy's colors

You are walking the trails
that declare this body
Abenaki land
and like the dream man
you are speaking my true name
Ndakinna

All Night She Dreams

All night she dreams
a panther, a white bear,
a wet moose.
When she wakes
she is on turtle's back.
She can feel the lumbering
movement beneath her.
Here she can talk to fire,
to stone, and people take
many shapes.
She knows that one day
her hips will grow heavy
as squash,
she will lie on the earth
and vines will grow
from her arms and legs,
milky kernels will form
on the ears of corn plants
growing skyward form her breasts.
Meanwhile, there is walking in balance,
there is clear thought,
and song
rising from her lips
like smoke, like mist,
like welcome clouds,
like some green and beautiful plant.

POETRY FROM ALICE JAMES BOOKS